War Room
to Victory

Other books by Raphael Grant:

Another Level of Prayer

Still Standing

Principles of Purpose and Adversity

Breaking Satanic Cycles

Strategic Prayer

Enemy at the Gate

War Room
to Victory

VICTORY WILL COST YOU SOMETHING

RAPHAEL GRANT

To order additional copies of this book, contact:
Xlibris
844-714-8691
www.Xlibris.com
Orders@Xlibris.com
830122

Contents

Sean and Sabitri, I want to thank you so much for your dedication to the type setting for this project, I highly appreciate you, the blessings will be endless.

I am dedicating this book to my boys Zuriel and Zephan,

I love you guys so much,you are my inspiration,

and also to you my queen, my best friend Aretha,

forever in love with you.

Chapter 1

Understand the Two Worlds

There are two worlds that all humanity operates within, the physical and the supernatural. There is a physical world that we experience with our senses (see, feel, touch) and a spiritual or supernatural world that our spirit operates within. As human beings, we were created to function and exist in both worlds simultaneously because we are both flesh and spirit. In other words, our physical body is specifically designed to function in this world (Earth), and our spirit is explicitly designed to operate in the spiritual world. Our flesh dwells or resides in the physical world, also known as the physical realm. Our spirit can only operate or function in the spiritual world or spiritual realm. In the physical realm, we have possessions that are required for us to function effectively such as food, clothes, houses, cars, etc. In the spiritual realm, we have the power to speak and declare God's word against the kingdom of darkness because the battle is not of the flesh but of the spirit. Ephesians 6:12 states, "For we do not wrestle against flesh and blood, but against principalities, against powers, against the rulers of the darkness of this age, against spiritual hosts of wickedness in the heavenly places."

God is not a man, he is a sovereign spirit that dwells above the heavens and has absolute dominion over the spiritual realm. All activity and decisions that God permits occur in the spiritual realm first, then it will manifest in the physical realm. You must be vigilant of what happens in the spiritual realm because when you go to sleep, it is your flesh that is resting, but your spirit is awake in another dimension. Dreams are the language of the Holy Spirit; he informs us of the things that will occur in the physical world. For example, have you ever experienced a dream that felt so real or you got injured in a dream and when you woke up, you had a scar or physical pain? This is a direct result of a demonic attack. If you are having demonic attacks in the spiritual world, those attacks will manifest in the physical world. Those attacks can negatively affect various aspects of your physical life such as marriage, finances, employment, business, your family, etc. Those of you that say, "I don't dream. I sleep like a little baby," you need deliverance. How can you contend with Satan and the kingdom of darkness if you don't have an insight into his kingdom? Until you prevail in the spiritual world, you cannot succeed in the physical world. You must understand these two worlds. Ephesians 1:21 says, "Far above all principality and power and might and dominion, and every name that is named, not only in this age but also in that which is to come."

Any spiritual activity that occurs in the spiritual realm that is not of God is called spiritual warfare. Spiritual warfare directly affects your mission, mandate, and assignment from God because evil entities are contending against you; they are trying to assassinate you and your family members. They are trying to take all your possessions and reduce you to nothing. Often believers question why trials and tribulations appear to occur in their lives. God has dominion over everything because he is the creator that was never created which means God can do anything He desires. God sent his only begotten son Jesus Christ to this Earth to be tried crucified and tested by the devil. The Bible says that Jesus experienced great physical affliction to include shame and reproach. When Jesus Christ was born the kingdom of darkness, King Herod was trying to kill him. If God allowed all these incidents to happen to Jesus, then why do we think our lives will be without pain and suffering? God allows pain and affliction to teach and make us stronger. If you have a personal relationship with Jesus and you follow ALL, the principles of God's word, you will prevail and be an overcomer like the son of man (Jesus). Luke 22:63–65 states, "Now the men who held Jesus mocked Him and beat Him. And having blindfolded Him, they struck Him on the face and asked Him, saying, 'Prophesy! Who is the one who struck You?' And many other things they blasphemously spoke against Him."

As a believer, if you are going to prevail in spiritual warfare and overcome the attacks of the kingdom of darkness (enemy), you must understand the two worlds (physical and spiritual). You cannot serve both kingdoms (Satan's kingdom, God's kingdom). You must choose one, and the other one will become your enemy. If you choose God's kingdom, then you have become an enemy of Satan. If you choose the Kingdom of Satan, then you have become an enemy of God. You cannot be neutral, in between, or lukewarm. If you are an enemy of God, you will suffer endless affliction in your physical life, and on the day of judgment, you will be condemned and thrown into the lake of fire which is the second death. Revelation 20:14 states, "Then Death and Hades were cast into the lake of fire. This is the second death."

The realm of the physical is the domain of the devil. That is why Jesus called the devil the prince of this world. How did the devil take possession of the physical world or the physical realm? In the beginning, when the Earth was created, Adam was given dominion by God over the Earth. God partnered with him to govern the Earth to accomplish God's divine agenda. God told Adam and Eve (Adam's helper) that they could eat anything in the Garden of Eden except the fruit from the tree of knowledge of good and evil. Adam and Eve disregarded God's command and committed treason against him by eating from the tree of knowledge of good and evil. As a result of Adam's actions, the dominion and authority over the Earth were transferred to Satan until Jesus was crucified and resurrected; his blood reconciled the Earth back to man. Adam's disobedience is the origin of sin which affects the world presently. Genesis 3:6 says, "So when the woman saw that the tree was good for food, that it was pleasant to the eyes, and a tree desirable to make one wise, she took of its fruit and ate. She also gave to her husband with her, and he ate."

Because Adam directly violated God's command and by doing so, he handed over the keys to the physical world to the devil. That is why the devil had the audacity to offer the kingdom of the physical world to Jesus in exchange for his soul. Jesus did not challenge or dispute Satan's authority for it is written in the scriptures that he possesses the authority over the physical world. Luke 4:6 says, "And the devil said to Him, "All this authority I will give You, and their glory; for this has been delivered to me, and I give it to whomever I wish.""

Satan's control over the physical world is the primary reason why we (believers in Jesus Christ) are attacked ferociously because our physical body dwells in the physical world. We live in this world, but we are not of this world; our citizenship is in heaven. This world is void of God, Christ, holiness, purity, and everything that is associated with God. The Bible refers to us as ambassadors of this Earth on behalf of Christ, we are representatives of our kingdom (spirit realm) here on the Earth. Second Corinthians 5:20 says, "Now then, we are ambassadors for Christ, as though

God were pleading through us: we implore you on Christ's behalf, be reconciled to God."

The Bible admonishes us that we cannot be friends with the world because the world is overwhelmed with detestable sin and evil. God respects principles, character, and obedience; he despises evil and sin. The Earth is engulfed with sinful people such as liars, murderers, pornographers, rapists, bigots, fornicators, and idol worshipers. Believers should not associate with people that are not of God because they can persuade us to sin. James 4:4 says, "Adulterers and adulteresses! Do you not know that friendship with the world is enmity with God? Whoever therefore wants to be a friend of the world makes himself an enemy of God."

Satan is the commander of the physical world that is why believers pray (decree and declare) to let God's will be done on earth (the physical world) as it is in heaven (the supernatural realm, the supernatural world, God's Kingdom) because we desire God's greatness, power, love, and his peace to manifest on the Earth. We live in this world, but we don't conform to the wickedness (murder, deceit, treachery, insurrection) of this world. We live by the standard of heaven which means we follow and adhere to the word of God. Matthew 6:10 says, "Your kingdom come. Your will be done on earth as it is in heaven."

The Bible teaches us to walk and live in the heavenly realm which is our residence. So as a believer, when we have supernatural encounters, it shouldn't be strange; it should be natural to us because we dwell in the heavenly and the earthly realm simultaneously. The reason why we get so excited about miracles, signs, and wonders is because we don't understand the heavenly world in which we live and operate in. Jesus said that signs shall follow them that believe. What it simply means is those that have been translated from the kingdom of darkness to the kingdom of light (acceptance of Jesus Christ as your Lord and Savior), these miracles, signs, and wonders naturally follow them. They will not struggle for it because it is a part of their normal life. Until you believe, you cannot live in the supernatural kingdom in the spirit world. Mark 16:17 says, "And these signs will follow those who believe: In My name they will cast out demons; they will speak with new tongues."

What affects others who are worldly (sinful, scornful) will not affect the righteous because we are not of this world. There are many different afflictions (disease, murder, persecution) that Satan has inflicted upon us, but if we stay focused on Jesus Christ, we will overcome the trials and tribulations of this world. You must understand the two worlds. John 16:33 states, "These things I have spoken to you, that in Me you may have peace. In the world you will have tribulation; but be of good cheer, I have overcome the world."

When you understand the two worlds you walk in confidence, you live audaciously. You are not intimidated or afraid of anything because you possess the power in Jesus Christ to prevail. If you don't understand the two worlds you will live a confused and frustrated life which God did not ordain for you. God created you to live a successful and abundant life to serve him faithfully. Joshua said as for me and my house we are for signs and wonders. I laid before you two worlds, blessings and curses, choose one. The world that destroys and the world that builds, choose one. The world that causes sickness, disease, and infirmity and the world that heals, builds, and reconciles, choose one. As for me and the household, I have chosen blessings, the supernatural kingdom, the kingdom of light, the kingdom of our God. As a believer, when you understand the two worlds, you will not act and conduct yourself (lie, cheat, steal, use profanity, gossip, hurt your brothers and sisters) as the physical world does. If you earnestly seek the kingdom of God first and abide by his word and his will, you will not fear the trials and calamity of this world. Always remember Jehovah has the final say over everything. Joshua 8:34 says, "And afterward he read all the words of the law, the blessings and the cursing, according to all that is written in the Book of the Law."

Chapter 2

Know Your Enemy

There are people who dislike God and rejoice in wickedness and that is why the Bible says let God arise and let his enemies be scattered. So if God has enemies, then you as a believer and a child of God will have enemies. One of the most tragic things is that we know that we have enemies but we don't know who they are and that can be devastating. It is like going to battle against an unknown foe without any knowledge or strategic plans. It is nearly impossible to succeed in the physical realm if you lack revelation. You must pray first and seek divine wisdom from God regarding your enemy. In addition, you must take an offensive stance by studying and learning everything (strengths, weaknesses, mannerisms, and habits) about your enemy to see the move of

God. For example, a boxer watches and studies videos of their opponents' previous fights to learn their strengths and weaknesses to gain an advantage in the fight. By obtaining this knowledge, you know exactly how your enemy will react; therefore, you can counteract their advances and prevail over them. Psalm 68:1 states, "Let God arise; Let His enemies be scattered; Let those also who hate Him flee before Him."

Jesus told his disciples to anticipate deliberate attacks from the enemy because of his name. You must understand that if you are a child of God, you will have enemies, and people will despise you regardless of what you do (right or wrong). Some people hate you because of your physical characteristics (too tall, short, light skin, dark skin, long hair, short hair, Indian, black, white) or difference in political or religious affiliation. Whatever the reason is, someone will not like you because you don't share the same opinion or belief system as they do. And that is why the ungodly will resent the godly, the impure will despise the pure, the ordinary will resent the extraordinary, but that is how life is designed. You cannot fulfill your dreams, goals, divine assignments, and mandates without having an enemy. Your enemy is part of the package. Matthew 10:22 says, "And you will be hated by all for My name's sake. But he who endures to the end will be saved."

Oftentimes you may not know what you are capable of, but your enemy will reveal your strengths and weaknesses. Gideon wasn't confident in himself; he didn't know who he was but the angel said to him that you are a mighty man of valor. He responded to the angel and said that "if I am a mighty man of valor then what am I doing hiding on the farm?" God wanted him to know that he is a mighty man of valor so God sent him to the camp of the enemy to discover himself. Judges 6:12 says, "And the Angel of the LORD appeared to him, and said to him, 'The Lord is with you, you mighty man of valor!'"

When he entered the camp of the enemy, there were two people that were discussing a dream that one of the men had dreamt. And after telling the other person about his dream, this was the response, "The bread that you saw that tumbled into the camp of the Midianites is not actually bread, but the sword of Gideon." The Lord has delivered the Midianites and the whole camp to Gideon. Your enemy revealed who you are! Judges 17:13–15 states, "And when Gideon had come, there was a man telling a dream to his companion. He said, 'I have had a dream: To my surprise, a loaf of barley bread tumbled into the camp of Midian; it came to a tent and struck it so that it fell and overturned, and the tent collapsed.' Then his companion answered and said, 'This is nothing else but the sword of Gideon the son of Joash, a man of Israel! Into his hand God has delivered Midian and the whole camp.' And so it was, when Gideon heard the telling of the dream and its interpretation, that he worshiped. He returned to the camp of Israel, and said, 'Arise, for the LORD has delivered the camp of Midian into your hand.'"

That attacks that come your way are an indication of the power that you are carrying in your spiritual womb. If you don't have enemies, battles, and warfare just know that you are a nonentity, not threatened by anybody. Whenever you are a threat to the kingdom of darkness, you will have enemies. Your threat level and the number of attacks that you receive will determine what you are carrying (power, presence of God) inside of you. There are many of you who are asking why am I going through so many attacks? The reason for the spiritual attacks is the oil on your head (the presence of God that is around you). The lesser the oil the lesser the attacks, the greater the oil the greater the attacks. The devil knows that if he doesn't continue to attack you that his kingdom will be in trouble, so that is why Satan has positioned his agents to attack you in different areas of your life (marriage, children, finances). The purpose of the enemies that have been planted into your life is to distract, frustrate, divide and conquer, thus reducing you to nothing. But I came to announce to somebody that your enemies are an indication that you are somebody and you are on the verge of receiving your transformation and breakthrough.

Giants in your life are not a sign of your exit from Egypt, but it is a sign and proof of your entry into Canaan. In other words, when you see more enemies coming up against you and you are having more battles and warfare, it means that you are about to stumble into your miracle. It means that something is about to explode in the heavens and manifest in the earth realm. It also means that your elevation is coming. It means that everything is coming to divine alignment concerning your destiny, life, purpose, and career. The devil will attack you when God is about to elevate you to the place that he has destined for you, so when the enemies are attacking you, it doesn't mean that you have sinned or you are living unrighteously. The enemies that are contending against you are indications of your stance of the anointing that is upon you. Your enemy is anybody that weakens your passion for the future.

An enemy is somebody who is more interested in discussing your past and not your future. The Bible says that "remember not the former things or consider the things of the old. Leave the past behind and look forward to your future because your greatness, victory, and ministry are ahead and not behind you." Anytime the enemy continuously reminds you of your past, it is an indication that they have lost track of your future and your destiny. Isaiah 43:18 says, "Do not remember the former things, nor consider the things of old."

There was an adulterous woman that was brought to Jesus, and men were getting ready to stone her to death because they despised her. Jesus stood there and observed the adulterous woman as the men were preparing to stone her to death. And when Jesus looked at her, he wasn't looking at her in the present time or what she had done in the past. Jesus was only looking ahead at her future. One stroke of mercy will wipe out all errors you have done in your past. Be careful of those that are persistent and consistent in discussing your past more than your future; they are your enemies. Parasites want what is in your hands, but prodigies desire what is in your heart. Every enemy is a parasite; they want to take what is in your hand but no enemy can take what God has given to you. John

7:10–11 says, "When Jesus had raised Himself up and saw no one but the woman, He said to her, 'Woman, where are those accusers of yours? Has no one condemned you?' She said, 'No one Lord.' And Jesus said to her, 'Neither do I condemn you; go and sin no more.'"

Jesus said that "you are sheep but you will find yourselves in the midst of wolves. Enemies will surround you." There are enemies all around to prevent you from succeeding in your career, relationship, and marriage. There are enemies whose assignment, mission, and mandate are attacked in various aspects of your life (finance, marriage, children, career, ministry) and bring you to a place of disgrace. So there are enemies everywhere. Your enemy could be the devil, spiritual entities, or human beings. Don't deceive yourself into thinking that your enemies are only spirits. Jesus told his disciples to never think that there will be no opposition or resistance. Jesus was giving his disciples foresight that there will be enemies and opposition along the way and to recognize and deal with them speedily. Matthew 10:16–17 states, "'Behold, I send you out as sheep in the midst of wolves. Therefore, be wise as serpents and harmless as doves. [17] But beware of men, for they will deliver you up to councils and scourge you in their synagogues.'"

When God opens a door for you and gives you a breakthrough and you tell somebody and the person is not happy for you, that person is an enemy. When great things are happening in your life and God is giving you one testimony after another and you are sharing the testimony with another person and he or she is not responding Hallelujah and Amen, that person is an enemy. Sometimes your enemies hire other enemies to target and frustrate you. In the book of Ezra, the native people hired counselors against the people of Judah to frustrate their purpose of rebuilding the temple because they did not like the accelerated progress that was occurring. The hired counselors were accusing the people of things they have not done. So they wrote letters to the Persian government to stop them from building the temple. Sometimes when you are accused people tend to believe the accusations that are written against you which is designed to become a stumbling block to hinder your progress. Ezra 4:4–5 states, "Then the people of the land tried to discourage the people of Judah. They troubled them in building, and hired counselors against them to frustrate their purpose all the days of Cyrus king of Persia, even until the reign of Darius king of Persia."

You are not supposed to fear your enemy. Your enemy is not designed for you to fear him or her. Your enemies have the ability to afflict the flesh and the body but they don't have the power and ability to afflict the soul, and that is why the Bible said, "Don't fear your enemies." It doesn't matter how many have come up against you, they can't kill you. Oftentimes what you are afraid of, they are afraid of you because if they weren't afraid of you, they will not focus so much time planning and scheming how to trap and bring you down. The kingdom of darkness will have a meeting just for one person, and that person could be you. Principalities and spiritual hosts of wickedness, territorial spirits, familiar spirits will gather in unison because of one person. But you cannot be scared of that witch that is living next door to you even though she planning to bring you down. She is just setting a trap for herself to fall into. Don't be afraid of the enemy. God Almighty has you in the palm of his hands. Matthew 10:28 says, "And do not fear those who kill the body but cannot kill the soul. But rather fear Him who is able to destroy both soul and body in hell."

Without enemies, you are yet to arrive at your destination. That is why Jesus lived thirty-three years on planet Earth, and for thirty of those years, he was quiet. But when he showed up, there were so many enemies, and the purpose of those enemies was to kill him. And in three years they killed him. But they thought that killing him will prevent him from getting to his destination, but they didn't know that killing him was the destination. That is why the Bible says that if the devil had known, he wouldn't have killed the king of glory. If you don't have enemies, you are yet to arrive at your destination. Know your enemy! First Corinthians 2:8 says, "Which none of the rulers of this age knew; for had they known, they would not have crucified the Lord of glory."

Chapter 3

How to Deal with Your Enemy and End Your Battle

There are so many of you that have unending battles that you are fighting year after year that won't stop, regardless of what you do. You have fasted and agonized in prayer against the satanic attacks, but the warfare is still ongoing. It seems that the more you pray and fast the more the battle intensifies, so you have concluded that maybe you were born to fight this battle or some who want to be extra spiritual use this terminology "this is my cross, I need to carry it." It is abnormal for you to have constant battles one after the other with no apparent conclusion because it contradicts God's word that you shall have peace. Numbers 6:26 says, "The LORD lift up His countenance upon you, And give you peace."

The battle has been in your life for so long that people ridicule and make a mockery of you. Your enemies are saying that God has forsaken and rejected you, and there is no hope or elevation for you. You have concluded that the battle is a generational battle, so nothing will work for you. Who told you that generational battles don't end, why should you fight your ancestor's battles? You must take a stance and deal with the enemy for the battle to end. Plasm 3:2–3 states, "Many are they who say of me, 'There is no help for him in God.' But You, O LORD, are a shield for me, My glory and the One who lifts up my head."

One of the saddest things is that many have tried to deal with their issues with praying and fasting and nothing changes. For you to obtain results, the prayers must be born out of revelation. If you have an issue with your marriage (arguing and fighting with your spouse) and you began to pray for restoration but the issues are not improving, then you must seek guidance from the Holy Spirit to receive revelation and the origin of the issue. For example, you and your spouse are trusting God for the fruit of the womb (a child) with no success. You went to the doctor to get a complete physical examination and the doctor gave both of you a clean bill of health which means your issues are not of the flesh (physical) but spiritual (satanic attack). You must petition God to reveal exactly who or what specific satanic force is preventing you from having a child. The source of the problem could be a jealous friend, coworker, or maybe a family member. Once the Holy Spirit reveals the source of the problem, you can pray strategically to overturn the situation in your favor. Until you are cognizant of the source of the contention, your breakthrough will not come to fruition.

What the enemy is doing to you is a crime. Why is it a crime? It is a crime because the Bible clearly states, "Touch not my anointed." Oftentimes people think that when the Bible says touch not my anointed, it is specifically for pastors, evangelists, prophets, apostles, or bishops but that is not the case. When you are a born-again believer and have a relationship with Christ, you are the anointed of the Lord. So when the Bible says touch not my anointed and do my prophets no harm, the Bible is talking about you. So anytime Satan or his agents touch you wrongfully, that person has broken the law; therefore, he is a criminal. Psalm 105:15 says, "Do not touch My anointed ones, And, do My prophets no harm."

When the Bible says touch not my anointed, it is also referring to everything that concerns us, our marriages, our relationships, our children, career, finance, health, glory, and ministry. If the enemy harms us in any fashion, it is a crime and will be punished by the court of heaven. Satan understands the scriptures better than we do, and he knows that he will be punished for all attacks against the righteous. Satan attempted to harm Jesus Christ. Satan said that "it is written jump from the pinnacle of the temple and fall, your feet will not dash against a stone because angels will take charge over you." He was quoting scripture. Jesus responded by saying the scriptures also say, "Don't tempt the Lord your God." As Christians, we must know the scriptures to avoid being deceived by Satan. Psalm 91:11–12 says. "For He shall give His angels charge over you, To keep you in all your ways. In their hands they shall bear you up, Lest you dash your foot against a stone."

It is critical that you execute judgment upon your enemy speedily; if not, your battle will be unending. Moses didn't want to return to Egypt so he provided numerous excuses to the Almighty God that he cannot speak with authority and confidence because he stutters. It was not because of a speech impediment; he was afraid for his life because he had killed a man, and the Egyptian leadership issued an order to terminate his life. God never responded or said anything about his excuse. God said, "Those who have plotted to execute you, I have finished them. You don't have any cause to be afraid of them." God executed judgment swiftly, quickly, and expeditiously because if God didn't execute judgment on these people, Moses's divine agenda and purpose and the prophetic word concerning the children of the Israelites would not have come into fruition and manifestation. Exodus 2:15 states, "When Pharaoh heard of this matter, he sought to kill Moses. But Moses fled from the face of Pharaoh and dwelt in the land of Midian; and he sat down by a well."

God will not do anything for you until you ask him. There are many of us who are waiting on God to execute judgment, but God is waiting on us to execute judgment because he has given us the authority and power to eliminate the enemy. When the sentence against the ungodly is not executed speedily by the righteous, the enemy will become bolder and begin to attack other aspects of your life because the enemy was not punished for the first offense. The devil feels that he is at liberty to continue doing evil, and that is when the battle becomes long and unending. They attack your health and nothing was done to them so they move to your finances, family, career, and this process continues until they reduce you to nothing and suddenly you are fighting multiple battles at the same time. Pretty soon you have become battle weary because you didn't punish the enemy speedily. Luke 9:1 states, "Then He called His twelve disciples together and gave them power and authority over all demons, and to cure diseases."

There are some of you who are saying that I don't have to deal with the ungodly in that manner because I want to allot time for them to repent but there are some evildoers that will never repent. For example, you are praying for Satan to repent. Nonsense, Satan will never repent! There are people who hate you without a cause and are determined to see you in pain and anguish. They will never change regardless of what you do, so you must terminate the enemy before they annihilate you. Ecclesiastes 8:11 says, "Because the sentence against an evil work is not executed speedily, therefore the heart of the sons of men is fully set in them to do evil."

There is greatness in you, the favor of God is upon you, but it is not manifesting because you have not dealt with the enemy quickly. When judgment is passed swiftly upon the wicked and they are buried, their memory is erased; nobody remembers them. But for that to happen, you must act quickly and urgently. As believers, we have no idea of the power, authority, and dominion that have been given to us by our Lord Jesus Christ. Jesus said, "I have given you the power to trample upon serpents and scorpions and over the enemy." Luke 10:19 says, "Behold, I give you the authority to trample on serpents and scorpions, and over all the power of the enemy, and nothing shall by any means hurt you."

There must be a season of peace, tranquility, serenity, quietness in your life to enjoy God's presence and blessings. King David, a ferocious warrior, had unending physical and spiritual warfare from every direction during his lifetime. King David had so much blood on his hands from his numerous battles and warfare that God would not permit him to build his temple in Jerusalem because God's temple represents purity and holiness. Even with all the fighting and battling that King David endured, there was a time in his life that he had to rest on every side. First King 5:4 says, "But now the LORD my God has given me rest on every side; there is neither adversary nor evil occurrence."

Anybody that is secretly in your life but that person is your problem, I decree that you will trample upon them. The spirit of the Lord will expose them, their activities will be scattered, their plans will be aborted, their intentions will be miscarried, and they will go into their graves quickly. You must end your battle quickly and decisively without any form of hesitation or procrastination. In Jesus's name, we pray. Amen.

Chapter 4

Shattering Monitoring Spirits

We cannot be ignorant of the devices of the enemy because someone is always observing us. Some of you may say, "I keep to myself and mind my own business. I don't interfere in other peoples' lives, so I don't expect anyone to intrude in my affairs." Satan has strategically positioned entities (people and spiritual beings) to interfere and cause turmoil in your life. You may be familiar with certain people that are observing you (friend, supervisor, relative); however, a monitoring spirit can also assume any physical form (fly, dog, a bird) so it is difficult to detect spiritual monitoring entities. You must pray and fast to receive revelation (divine information) from God to recognize and prevail over the enemy. Second Corinthians 2:11 says "Lest Satan should take advantage of us; for we are not ignorant of his devices."

The agents of the devil are interfering with your life, destiny, career, marriage, family, and everything that concerns you with a mechanism called monitoring. They observe and monitor every move in your life to cause division and misdirection which will result in affliction. When a monitoring spirit pursues you, they themselves are not doing the dirty work of attacking you; their assignment is to watch your daily routine (bedtime, habits, work schedule) and report the information to their superior. Their superior is the one that is using the information against you, and that is how monitoring spirits operate. However, there are rare occasions that the person that is conducting the monitoring is the same individual that is trying to destroy you.

Monitoring spirits are real entities and not figments of our imagination as we pray and fast remember that somebody is always watching and tracking us to make sure that we remain stagnant. If you begin to pay attention, you will notice that there is one particular area of your life that there is constant contention. When you think that the door has finally opened for you for that dream job, fruit of the womb (child), or a new home, you will notice that something always seems to derail your plans. For example, they may be observing your marriage to see if it is going well, and if so, they are plotting against you to cause confusion to break up your marriage. Suddenly you and your spouse will begin to argue about trivial things and cannot agree on anything. The monitoring agent has sent this information to their superior (boss) to attack you and ensure there is no accomplishment, achievement, fulfillment, and satisfaction in your relationship.

The agents of the devil initiate evil in every part of your life because of jealously. The enemy knows that God is blessing you, and they will continue to inflict stress and suffering in every aspect of your life to cause you to doubt God. Why does a wicked and a troublesome man walk with a perverse or willful mouth? The answer is very simple, to report to his superior everything he has observed in the areas of your life in which God has uplifted and prospered you. Also, it is to create confusion and problems in your life, which will intensify your battles and warfare. Proverbs 6:12–14 states, "A worthless person, a wicked man, walks with a perverse mouth; He winks with his eyes, He shuffles his feet, He points with his fingers; Perversity is in his heart, He devises evil continually, He sows discord."

There are some of you that recognize that you are under demonic and satanic surveillance. You can literally sense somebody is watching and following you, and when you turn around, you don't see anybody. Sometimes you notice a bird, a cat, or dog that follows you; these animals are monitoring devices that are planted to keep you in perpetual affliction. Just when you think that your business is increasing financially your employee quits, your machine malfunctions or your business is facing bankruptcy. That contract that you worked so hard to obtain, and you were confident that you won suddenly; they have changed their mind. The monitoring spirits saw that you won that contract, and they reversed the decision in the spiritual realm because of jealousy and selfishness. They knew that this contract will bless and enhance your life; therefore, they had purpose and determination to take it from you. Beware of monitoring spirits. If you don't blind and shut them down, they will shut you down. Who is monitoring you? Who is that person that doesn't want to see your progress? Who is that person that is following you around and recording your strengths and your weaknesses?

Monitoring spirits are wicked and troublesome spirits, and their purpose is to create unrest in your life. Every good thing that comes into your life, they uproot and remove it. They observe and monitor you at work. If you get a promotion, they create a storm and remove your name from the list. In the book of Daniel, how did King Nebuchadnezzar know that Shadrach, Meshach, and Abed-Nego would not bow to an idol (false God)? In those days Babylon was a superpower nation of our world, so you can imagine the responsibilities and the duties that was on the shoulders of King Nebuchadnezzar, so he didn't have time to follow these three young men to see if they complied with his law (bow and worship his God only). This is what occurred. Somebody followed them, observed them, and reported their findings to the king that they were not complying with the law because they worshiped the one and true God, Jehovah. You must pray and be watchful. Don't tell people all of your personal situations; they may use it against you. Again, the people that are closest to you could be the enemy. Be vigilant always. Daniel 3:12 states, "There are certain Jews whom you have set over the affairs of the province of Babylon: Shadrach, Meshach, and Abed-Nego; these men, O king, have not paid due regard to you. They do not serve your gods or worship the gold image which you have set up."

You are being observed, you are being watched, and they are following you around in your dreams. They are monitoring you both spiritually and physically because they don't want your happiness and joy. They watch when you are going to write that exam. You have studied and know that you are going to pass because you have worked so hard. But the enemy wants to frustrate you; they cause you to fail the exam by two or three points. So you are repeating the exam for a decade with no success. They can monitor others but not you or your family, and the only way we can prevent this from occurring is to release judgment upon them.

Judas Iscariot was waiting and watching for an occasion to betray Jesus. How could he find an occasion without observing and monitoring? It doesn't mean that Judas Iscariot wasn't with Jesus; he was the treasurer of the ministry and the last person Jesus spoke with before he retired to bed, but he was still monitoring and he sought an opportunity to betray and nail him

(Jesus) to his cross. Judas gave a sign to his conspirators by kissing Jesus on his cheek. Matthew 26:14–16 states, Then one of the twelve, called Judas Iscariot, went to the chief priests and said, "What are you willing to give me if I deliver Him to you?" And they counted out to him thirty pieces of silver. So from that time he sought opportunity to betray Him."

There are some people in your life that you think truly loves and cares about you; you believe in your heart that they are your friends and confidants, but they are actually on assignment against you. They are walking and moving with you every step of the way, but they are like Judas Iscariot looking for an opportunity to nail you to the cross. Some of them are far away from your village, the hometown, or the country where you were born, but they are still monitoring you because monitoring spirits don't need plane tickets to come to you. They don't need to drive their vehicles either. Sometimes when they are watching from far away, they will position a person that is close to you to watch and observe you. So you think that when they (friend or relative) call and ask you how are you doing, how is the family, husband, job, or school, they actually care about your well-being, it is a lie; they are waiting for a response and the response is actually the information that they needed. They may even throw Christian jargon in their conversation (the Lord is great, God is good, I had a dream or vision about you) to make you comfortable because that is the language that attracts your attention. For example, last week you spoke to your confidant about your finances being depleted and they responded by saying, "I am praying for you and I am believing God for your recovery" and because he or she used God in the conversation, you quickly open up and provide all the information that they are seeking. Beloved, please beware of these types of deceptions that the enemy will utilize against you.

Monitoring spirits want to see your downfall so they must be shut down immediately.

Often times when they are doing their bidding, they think nobody is seeing them, not even God. And the reason why they believe so is because they are not punished for their evil deeds; judgment is not coming upon them so they continue to execute their diabolical schemes. But I am here to announce to you, not this time around because the Lord has promised to bless and lift us up. The Lord has vowed to fulfill his promises in our lives. The Lord has guaranteed us that he will do a new thing in our lives. And anybody that opposes, resists, or rises up against us will meet their untimely death. The Bible says that the scepter of the wicked should not fall on the land of the righteous, it is an abomination, it is prohibited, it cannot happen that is why anybody that is following you around if they don't cease, they will be buried in their graves speedily. Psalm 125:3 states, "For the scepter of wickedness shall not rest on the land allotted to the righteous, Lest the righteous reach out their hands to iniquity."

Any spirit or person assigned to monitor you, today I shut them down. When they look for you, they will not find or locate you. Any group of people or any individual positioned to follow you around, I declare in the name of Jesus let the earth which they walk upon open thy mouth and swallow them up. Let sudden judgment and affliction enter their dwelling, let them go down quickly, let them be buried, let them be cut off prematurely, and let them fall into the pit that they dug for us. Father, let them become victims of their own curse words. Father, strike them with disease and infirmity that has no cure. Let disaster overtake them suddenly. Beloved, always remember that you must fast. Pray consistently and walk in the integrity of God's word and principles in order to blind and defeat monitoring spirits. Amen! Proverbs 6:15 says, "Therefore his calamity shall come suddenly; Suddenly he shall be broken without remedy."

Chapter 5

Use the Earth as a Spiritual Warfare

God created and spoke to earth as a living entity. God said let the earth bring forth living creatures according to its kind (cattle, birds). If God spoke to the earth, it means that the earth has ears. If the earth has ears, then it means that the earth also has eyes, nose, mouth, and other parts. If the earth did not have ears, then God wouldn't have spoken to it. God spoke to the earth and told the earth what he wants the earth to produce. The earth listened to what God said and produced according to what God had commanded. God didn't treat the earth as an inanimate object but as a living entity that can speak and hear. Genesis 1:24 says, "Then God said, 'Let the earth bring forth the living creature according to its kind: cattle and creeping thing and beast of the earth, each according to its kind'; and it was so."

God commanded and exercised his authority over the earth. God provided specific instructions to the earth; he did not provide the earth a choice whether to obey or not. When it comes to the language of the spirit, there is no debate or dialogue like the physical earthly realm where we have dialogue, consensus, and compromise. The things of the spirit and the things of the supernatural, the language that they understand are commands, authority, and power. In other words, in order to get results in the spirit and the supernatural world, you must command, exercise authority and dominion.

Anytime you sense a demonic force, a satanic force, or a territorial spirit that is occupying your space, you cannot address those evil entities tenderly such as "Spirit, please depart from my dwelling." If you address the satanic beings as such, they will torment you forever. To obtain results, you must use strong commands such as "You foul spirit, I dislodge, dispossess, and disarm you from my dwelling place in the name of Jesus Christ." The spirit has no choice but to oblige because the only language that the spirit understands is dominion, power, and authority.

When God was speaking to the earth, he commanded the earth to be fruitful and multiply and replenish the earth and subdue it. Subdue means to command and use the earth to its maximum potential and because the earth has ears, the earth listened and obeyed the commands. If we have control of the earth and God has put us in charge of the earth, then it means that whatever we say to the earth. The earth must accommodate us because the earth is under our dominion. Because of ignorance, we have no idea the value of the earth. All we know is that the earth was created for us to dwell in and use the natural resources to build a business, homes, and harvest (farming). Often people misinterpret the scripture that says, "Be fruitful and multiply." We typically associate this verse of scripture with procreation (producing children). The scripture also means to be productive and use the earth (natural resources, land, water) to increase our wealth and prosperity. By not understanding the earth's true purpose, we are only utilizing a fraction of the earth. Genesis 1:27–28 states, "So God created man in his own image, in the image of God created he him; male and female created he them. And God blessed them, and God said unto them, be fruitful, and multiply, and replenish the earth, and subdue it: and have dominion over the fish of the sea, and over the fowl of the air, and over every living thing that moveth upon the earth."

The earth is a weapon that we can use in spiritual warfare to advance the purposes of God concerning our lives. But until you understand and come in contact with that revelation (divine information from God), you will be unable to use it to your full advantage. There are certain people that use the earth for their benefit in battle and spiritual warfare. Even God used the earth for spiritual warfare. When the children of the Israelites were in Egyptian captivity and God sent Moses to deliver the children of the Israelites out of Egyptian imprisonment. One of the plagues that God used against the Egyptians was the ground. God instructed Moses to strike the ground (earth), and when Moses struck the ground, lice began to come out of the ground. The earth produced the lice to afflict the Egyptians, but the children of the Israelites were not affected. The earth has eyes because if the earth didn't have eyes the lice would have afflicted the children of the Israelites because they were also living in the same land as the Egyptians. But because the earth has eyes, it was able to differentiate between the Israelites and the Egyptians. Exodus 8:16–19 says, "So the Lord said to Moses, 'Say to Aaron,

"Stretch out your rod, and strike the dust of the land, so that it may become lice throughout all the land of Egypt.'" And they did so. For Aaron stretched out his hand with his rod and struck the dust of the earth, and it became lice on man and beast. All the dust of the land became lice throughout all the land of Egypt. Now the magicians so worked with their enchantments to bring forth lice, but they could not. So, there were lice on man and beast. Then the magicians said to Pharaoh, 'This is the finger of God.' But Pharaoh's heart grew hard, and he did not heed them, just as the Lord had said."

Using the earth as a weapon is so powerful to the extent that Jesus told his disciples, "When you go and preach and you enter into a new house to propagate the gospel and they deny, refuse, and reject you, shake off the dust under your feet as a testimony against them." In other words, anyone who refused the word of the Lord their fate and blood are in their own hands; when the final judgment occurs, they will have no excuse because they were given an opportunity to choose eternal life but they refused. So now the earth became a witness against them. Mark 6:11 says, "And whoever will not receive you nor hear you, when you depart from there, shake off the dust under your feet as a testimony against them. Assuredly, I say to you, it will be more tolerable for Sodom and Gomorrah in the day of judgment than for that city!"

When it comes to witchcraft and satanic activities, sometimes the evil, wicked, *occultic*, and demonic people that want to tamper with your destiny, your life, and everything that concerns you, they look for your footprints on the ground. Wherever you have walked and there is a trail of your footprint, they collect it from the dust. What do they use it for when they collect the dust? They speak to the earth against you, then they throw it back unto the earth. And by the time you realize whatever they have spoken unto to the dust, the evil incantations begin to manifest and take root in your lives.

The earth is so powerful and resourceful that it has the ability to produce life, and it has the ability to take life. We, as human beings, were created from the dust of the earth. And when we die, we shall return to the dust of the earth. In other words, the earth is the womb of the living and the dead. A blind man came to Jesus to seek healing from his blindness. Jesus did not speak and rebuke the blindness; Jesus did not lay hands on the blind man. Jesus spat (spit) on the earth and anointed the eyes of the blind man with the clay from the earth. In other words, Jesus was using the earth to rebuke and to arrest the spirit of blindness and to command the spirit of blindness to return back to where he came from. John 9:6–7 says, "When He had said these things, He spat on the ground and made clay with the saliva; and He anointed the eyes of the blind man with the clay. And He said to him, 'Go, wash in the pool of Siloam' (which is translated, Sent). So, he went and washed, and came back seeing."

Korah rebelled against Moses. Korah had two hundred and fifty other followers, leaders of the congregation, who were saying that Moses was not the only prophet, that they also hear the voice of God. So they rebelled against Moses and they stood at one side separating themselves from Moses and his followers. The Bible said while Moses was speaking, the earth opened her mouth and swallowed them up. God used the earth as a weapon to swallow Moses's enemies (Korah and his followers), and there was no trace of them. The earth not only swallowed them as human beings but also their properties, their buildings, and anything that was connected to them. Numbers 16:32 says, "And the earth opened its mouth and swallowed them up, with their households and all the men with Korah, with all their goods."

Isaac went to a strange land and there was famine and drought in the land. The indigent (needy) didn't know what to do; they were suffering from hunger but the Bible says that when Isaac entered the same land that produced famine. He sowed seeds and in that same year. He received a hundredfold from the same barren land that wasn't producing or yielding any harvest. The difference between Isaac and the indigent is a revelation because it was the same land and the same seed that was planted by Isaac. You can speak and get results from the earth concerning your destiny, business, children, family, and all your endeavors because the ground is a living entity that listens when you speak to it. Genesis 26:1, 12–13 says, "There was a famine in the land, besides the first famine that was in the days of Abraham. And Isaac went to Abimelech king of the Philistines, in Gerar. Then Isaac sowed in that land, and reaped in the same year a hundredfold; and the LORD blessed him. The man began to prosper, and continued prospering until he became very prosperous."

Joshua said, "I command the heavens and the earth to be a witness." How do they bear witness? Isaiah said, "Hear O heavens, and give ear, O earth," in other words, listen and pay attention to what I am saying. Isaiah was not only speaking to the heavens but also to the earth. You must come to the place where you begin to speak to the earth and tell the earth that I don't like the distraction that is coming upon me. I don't like the calamity that is following me. I don't like the shame and the reproach that is coming to me. Let the contrary and the opposite start occurring in my life. I am not here to fail. I am not here to be a nonentity, and whatever I speak and declare to the earth will manifest for my advantage as long as I dwell on the earth. Deuteronomy 30:19 says, "I call heaven and earth as witnesses today against you, that I have set before your life and death, blessing and cursing; therefore, choose life, that both you and your descendants may live."

Jeremiah the prophet dealt with Jehoiakim by speaking to the earth and what he has spoken manifested. He said, "Earth, I declare that as long as Jehoiakim is walking on the earth, neither he nor his descendants will produce offspring nor prosper in any way." Jeremiah just dispossessed Jehoiakim, the king of Judah, and rendered him childless. And also declared that none of his descendants will rise up and sit on the throne of David. In other words, there is nobody from his linage that will become king after him. Jeremiah 22:29–30 states, "O earth, earth, earth, Hear the word of the LORD! Thus says the LORD: 'Write this man down as childless, A man who shall not prosper in his days; For none of his descendants shall prosper, sitting on the throne of David, and ruling anymore in Judah.'"

The authority in which God used to speak and create the earth is the same power and authority that has been given to man. God said he has given power and authority to man to subdue the earth. You must learn how to command and speak to the earth for your benefit. It has nothing to do with your physical location but everything to do with revelation. Because until you discover revelation, it doesn't matter where you move to, you will still have the same problems. But when you receive revelation from God, it doesn't matter which continent that you dwell in; the earth will labor for your prosperity. Those who are blessed and flourishing, they are no different from you. They have merely discovered a revelation that you have not contacted yet, but your time is coming.

If you understand the way the earth functions, then you can succeed, you can progress, you can excel, and you can advance if you use the earth to your advantage. You can speak to the ground and say, "As long I am living here on earth, I will not live in mediocrity. As long as I am walking on you, you shall work for my gain. Wherever I go, I will be accepted. I will not be denied, despised, and disdained. Wherever I go, I will be highly favored. Every blessing, goodness, kindness, and favor that is embedded in the earth will come to me. O earth, anybody that attempts to use you against me, let it not work. O earth, hear my voice and hear the voice of the Lord. I am a covenanted child of God and you [earth] must hear me. Anybody that attempts to deploy you [earth] against me, my destiny, my family, my ministry, and my career I decree let peace be far from them, let the judgment of fire consume them in Jesus's name. Amen!"

Chapter 6

Victory Will Cost You Something

Victory is sweet and joyous but it is not cheap. Being victorious and an overcomer will cost you something, and you must be ready to pay the price for it. Victory brings celebration and jubilation, but for you to have victory, there must be pain. Without resistance, opposition, battle, pain, and suffering, there is no victory. You can't be victorious without overcoming your opponent and your resistance. The bedrock of victory is battle and warfare; you don't just desire, wish or speak victory, but you must be ready to experience hardship. Jesus paid the price for our sins with his life. First Corinthians 15:57 says, "The sting of death is sin, and the strength of sin is the law. But thanks be to God, who gives us the victory through our Lord Jesus Christ."

Victory is already assured for believers in Jesus Christ; however, you must pay the price to see the visibility, the physicality, and the tangibility of your victory. We, believers, want to receive the benefit of the victory, but we don't want to work for it. For example, you want a breakthrough and favor with God, but you don't want to pray and fast or spend time in the presence of God. You want somebody else (pastor, friend) to petition God on your behalf for your breakthrough, it doesn't work that way because God wants you to have a relationship with him. John 3:16 says, "For God so loved the world that He gave His only begotten Son, that whoever believes in Him should not perish but have everlasting life."

We are living in a very difficult and challenging time due to COVID-19, health, career, and economic problems. There are many who have been laid off from their jobs, they are not progressing as they once did, but the Bible said for us to be victorious and overcomers, we must constantly operate in faith and not fear. We have read so many stories of people who have been victorious due to military power and might. We have even read through scriptures of how individuals and groups of people have been victorious because of their superiority over their opponents. And oftentimes, when you read or hear stories of conquest, it is very sweet and appealing to the ear, soul, and heart, but it will cost you something. The fact that God has promised you victory and said that he will bless and favor you doesn't mean that you will not have conflict. God promises to attract enemies, battle, and engage in warfare, and for you to defeat your opponent, your haters, and the resistance, you must understand that it will cost you something; you are defined by the opposition and the adversities that you overcome. First John 5:4 says, "For whatever is born of God overcomes the world. And this is the victory that has overcome the world—our faith."

To be victorious means that you have to overcome and prevail against something. In life you are defined by what people see around you externally, by the storm and the adversity that you are going through. People are speculating and whispering all kinds of things concerning you such as God has forgotten and rejected you based on your external circumstances. But people forget that sometimes you can have an external storm, but inside you, there is calmness and peace. Most people are impressed by your outer appearance, the way you dress, the car you drive, your career, the home you live in and have formed an opinion of you, but God doesn't see your outward appearance or the material things that you have acquired. He looks at the heart and soul. First Samuel 16:7 says, "But the LORD said to Samuel, 'Do not look at his appearance or at his physical stature, because I have refused him. For the LORD does not see as man sees; for man looks at the outward appearance, but the LORD looks at the heart.'"

Sometimes people cannot figure you out. They cannot understand why you remain calm through all your adversity because it will take someone with the same spirit as you to discern what is going on inside of you which is different from the outside. That is why the Bible said, "Greater is he that is in me than he that is in the world." So for victory to manifest, it is important to understand what is going on inside your mind, soul, and your spirit. If you don't have the victory internally, you cannot have the victory externally. If you have not overcome it internally, you cannot overcome it externally. First John 4:4 states, "You are of God, little children, and have overcome them, because He who is in you is greater than he who is in the world."

The Bible said that Mordecai sent a message to Ester and informed her of the plot that Haman planned against the entire Jewish race. Mordecai told Ester, "You have come into the kingdom for such a time as this," and Mordecai asked Ester to do something about the situation. Otherwise, God is going to raise another person to use instead of you. Ester understood the message and Ester responded to Mordecai and told Mordecai to declare a three-day fast among the entire Jewish race that she and her servants will also participate in. Then she said to Mordecai at the end of the three-day fast she would enter into the king's court without an invitation which was against the law. In those days entering the king's chambers without an invitation will cost you your life. But Ester said, "I am going to enter into the king's palace without an invitation and if I die, then I die." Victory was going to come, but it almost cost Ester her life so that her people could be free. She was willing to pay the price for victory. Ester 4:15–17 states, "Then Esther told them to reply to Mordecai: 'Go, gather all the Jews who are present in Shushan, and fast for me; neither eat nor drink for three days, night or day. My maids and I will fast likewise. And so, I will go to the king, which is against the law; and if I perish, I perish!' So Mordecai went his way and did according to all that Esther commanded him."

If your victory doesn't cost you anything, you cannot enjoy it; it is not sweet. For you to have victory and triumph, you must be ready to battle. As believers, we don't battle with guns, bombs, or swords. We battle on our knees in the war room through prayer in the name and blood of Jesus Christ. We battle with the potency of the scriptures. In other words, there are certain situations and circumstances that if you are going to have the victory, you must quote the scriptures against the resistance, against your enemies who don't want you to prevail and excel. You must be a student of the word and you must be loaded with the word, so when confronted with any situation and condition, you have a specific word to declare and decree and to use against that opposition. Philippians 4:13 says, "I can do all things through Christ who strengthens me."

Sometimes victory will cost you your reputation, friends, family, career, or business. Victory doesn't come on a silver platter. Victory is not inherited; you must work for it. Victory is not a gift; you must fight and contend for it if you want to break the generational curses that have been undermining the destiny of your life and ministry. Beloved, you must stand up and fight and be willing to lay down your life. Where are the Esters in this generation? Sometimes you must let go of food and drinks and instead stay in the place of prayer and fasting. Jesus said that there are some situations and conditions that you have to stay in fasting and prayers to achieve victory. The Bible says, "Pray without ceasing until you receive your miracle." Matthew 17:21 states, "However, this kind does not go out except by prayer and fasting."

If you are going to have victory, sometimes you must have sleepless nights. In other words, you must pray throughout the night. You must stand in the presence of the Almighty God and travail and agonize in prayer and hold on to the horns of the altar and his throne until you receive victory. Sometimes you have to quote the scriptures back to God and tell God that you believe in the scriptures and remind him that he exalted his word above his name, so let it manifest that which he has spoken in the scriptures concerning your life. Psalm 138:2 states, "I will worship toward your holy temple, and praise your name for your lovingkindness and your truth; for you have magnified your word above all your name."

If you don't battle now, your children will fight the battle that you didn't fight. If you don't stop this curse in your family, this cycle of defeat and failure will still be present. Your children and grandchildren will experience the same battle and warfare because you didn't rise up and eliminate the enemy speedily. Jesus left his heavenly estate and came to the earth to reconcile man back to God and to redeem humanity, and it cost him his life. He was ridiculed; they spat on him. He was rejected, despised, disdained. He was falsely accused, flogged, beaten, nailed, and let him carry his own cross; he died and was buried because that was required to achieve the victory. Matthew 27:30 says, "Then they spat on Him, and took the reed and struck Him on the head. [31] And when they had mocked Him, they took the robe off Him, put His own clothes on Him, and led Him away to be crucified."

We are not in this battle, warfare, and conquest by ourselves. We have the Lord Jesus Christ, our shepherd who is standing with us to ensure that we have the victory. The scriptures say that Jesus with be with us always even until the end of the age. You should be encouraged, motivated and excited. Remember, weeping might be endured for a night, but joy shall come in the morning. Pain, affliction, and stress have expiration dates. Those that have overcome (affliction, persecution of this world) shall receive peace and everlasting life from God. Matthew 28:20 says, "Teaching them to observe all things that I have commanded you; and lo, I am with you always, even to the end of the age." Amen.

How can you know God as a healer if you don't have the problem of sickness? How would you know him as the way if you have not been hindered by the demons of hell? How would you know him as a provider if your financial kingdom had never suffered violently? Sometimes you need to pay the price to have the victory. It is time to take a stance in prayer and decree and declare your progress, your advancement, your manifestation, your healing, your peace, your joy, blessing, and triumph in Jesus's name, Amen!

Chapter 7

Take Your Case to the Court of Heavens

There are two worlds that believers operate within, the heavenly realm (spiritual) and the earthly realm (physical). The earthly realm is a replica of the heavenly realm, so everything that occurs in heaven also occurs on the earth. There is a court in heaven where the Almighty God administers justice and a court on earth where judges administer justice. There are prosecutors and defense attorneys in the court of heaven just as there are in the court on the earth. As believers of Jesus Christ, we take our case to the court of heaven to receive justice because we are not of this world; our citizenship is in heaven. Therefore, we adhere to the rules and regulations of the Bible. Philippians 3:20 says, "For our citizenship is in heaven, from which we also eagerly wait for the Savior, the Lord Jesus Christ."

The Bible is the blueprint for life, and it contains all the answers to achieve success in the physical and spiritual realms. We must search the scriptures diligently for the solutions to all our problems or issues. For example, if you are having problems with your health, finances, or your children, there are specific scriptures that pertain to those issues. Once you locate the scriptures, you must pray, fast, and seek the Holy Spirit for guidance and understanding concerning the issues. The reason why many believers have lost battles is because they have never entered the spiritual war room. They attempted to solve their issues outside of the war room in the physical realm. Some of you want God and the angels to come down from heaven and drag you into the war room, but they will not force you to enter the war room. You must stop procrastinating and complaining about your conditions, circumstances and take your case to the court of heaven. We are not fighting against flesh and blood enemies but against spiritual forces of evil that dwell in the heavenly places. Ephesians 6:12 says, "For we do not wrestle against flesh and blood, but against principalities, against powers, against the rulers of the darkness of this age, against spiritual hosts of wickedness in the heavenly places."

The Almighty God is the judge of the court in heaven, so believers will always receive a verdict that is in line with the scriptures. Prophet Micaiah was given the privilege of witnessing the court of heaven in session. God the Almighty was sitting on his throne discussing the fate of King Ahab, the king of Israel. God rendered a verdict that King Ahab would die in battle. King Ahab was on his horse getting ready to go to battle at a place called Ramoth Gilead, a Levitical city and city of refuge east of the Jordan River (Josh. 20:8, 21:38). King Ahab had no idea that the court of heaven was in session deciding his fate at the time just as many believers today. first Kings 22:19–20 states, "Then Micaiah said, 'Therefore hear the word of the LORD: I saw the LORD sitting on His throne, and all the host of heaven standing by, on His right hand and on His left. And the LORD said, "Who will persuade Ahab to go up, that he may fall at Ramoth Gilead?" So, one spoke in this manner, and another spoke in that manner.'"

As a believer of Christ, when we seek justice, we must enter the war room and take our case (problems, issues) to the court of heaven and present it to God. The Lord Almighty God, the judge of all judges, said to argue your case and provide strong arguments and concrete facts. If you petition God for blessings, then you should provide strong evidence of why God should bless you. You must demonstrate that you have been faithful by walking in righteousness (not stealing, lying, gossiping, fornicating) and adhering to his laws and principles. For example, you must seek the kingdom of God first, pay your first fruit, tithes, and offering and honor and treat your neighbors as you treat yourself. So if you want to be blessed with a new house, a new job or to be married, you must be obedient in everything that you do and present your case as such to God because God will not reward the disobedient and any act that contradicts his word. Isaiah 41:21 says, "'Present your case,' says the LORD. 'Bring forth your strong reasons,' says the King of Jacob."

You have received a prophecy concerning a new successful business and a fruitful marriage. But years have passed and what was spoken over your lives has not manifested. You have been praying, fasting, walking in God's ways, honoring him with your tithes and service; you become confused, frustrated, and not certain on what course of action to take. You must take your case to the court of heaven, pray unto Jehovah, and remind him that what he has spoken must manifest because he is not a man that should lie neither the son of man that should repent. God exalts his word above his name. Psalm 138:2 states, "I will worship toward thy holy temple, and praise thy name for thy lovingkindness and for thy truth: for thou hast magnified thy word above all thy name."

You have this infirmity in your body that has created discomfort for years, and it is not going away. It is causing you so much pain and anguish that is making you depressed. Ask God if there is no balm in Gilead, is there no physician in Israel, is it not written, and has it not been said that you are the Almighty God, your name is Jehovah-Rapha, the Lord God that heals? Is it not written and have you not heard that by the stripes of Jesus that we are healed then why am I still suffering from this infirmity, disease, and sickness that will not let me be myself? Bring your case to the Almighty God, and have strong reasons why heaven should intervene for you. Isaiah 53:5 says, "But He was wounded for our transgressions, He was bruised for our iniquities; The chastisement for our peace was upon Him, And by His stripes we are healed."

You have been called by God; you have the oil of God on your life; you have been called into ministry, but things are difficult. God told you specifically that your calling is in ministry; he is going to use you to demonstrate his power and send you to the nations of our world to declare his counsel and to propagate (spread) the Gospel of Jesus Christ. But every door is shut. You are walking upright in the integrity of God's word; you are living in righteousness. The kingdom of darkness has issued a satanic injunction against your mandate and assignment. You must enter the war room, fast, and pray (decree/declare) vigorously for deliverance and breakthrough unto Jehovah and present your case to the court of heaven.

The Lord said that he will make your name great; he will make your voice echo around the world and that your name will be mentioned among the great men and women of the land, yet nobody knows you and nothing is happening. And there are some of you that have given up on what God has spoken concerning your life and destiny. You must bring the matter to the court of heaven, state your case, and give strong reasons why God must intervene to help you. Genesis 12:2 says, "I will make you a great nation; I will bless you and make your name great; And you shall be a blessing."

You are impoverished. You are in so much debt that you must borrow to survive. As a covenanted child of God, you were created to operate in abundance and overflow. God is obligated to supply all your needs because he is your shepherd, and the duties and responsibilities of a shepherd ate to take care of his sheep. Why are you operating in lack and suffering and why are you seeking justice? Present your evidence (living by the scriptures, having good character, being honest, faithful, obedient) to the court of heaven and ask God why your life contradicts everything that has been written in the scriptures (God's word). Proverbs 22:7 states, "The rich rules over the poor, And the borrower is a servant to the lender."

People ridicule and make a mockery of you because of your faithfulness to God and because of your service in the house of God. You have asked God to bless you so that the people will know that you are serving a living God, and those that follow and put their trust, hope, and faith in him will not be disappointed and nothing is happening. Take your case to the court of heaven and ask God, "Has it not been written that he, Jehovah, will perfect that which concerns us? In other words, his council for our lives, destiny, and everything that concerns us will stand unfailingly. Why is the manifestation not coming to fruition?" Make strong arguments and give strong reasons why your situations must turn around expediently (now)! Psalm 138:8 says, "The LORD will perfect that which concerns me; your mercy, O LORD, endures forever; Do not forsake the works of Your hands."

You are educated, you are brilliant, you are intelligent, you have all the degrees and the credentials, you have multiple PhDs, yet no organization, no company, no institution will hire you. When you send your resume, they review it and tell you that you are overqualified. When you reduce your credentials and your degrees on your resume, they tell you that you are underqualified. No company is hiring you and the Bible says, "He that doesn't work should not eat." So how does God expect you to eat and survive when you are not working? It is not because you are sluggish or lazy, but circumstances and situations will not allow you to excel and to progress. And there are some of you because you have been through these trials continuously, you have come to accept that this is how your life is supposed to be. No! This is not how your life is supposed to be. Your life is not glorifying God; it is not setting the example of bringing people into the kingdom. That is why you must pray forcefully and take the matter to the court of heaven. Quote the scriptures unto Jehovah and say, "I am not leaving your presence until you overturn my situation and impart blessings on my life." Second Thessalonians 3:10 says, "For even when we were with you, we commanded you this: If anyone will not work, neither shall he eat."

You are writing (taking the test) the same board exam continuously, but you are not passing; you have studied for months and you know the material, yet you are still unsuccessful. The Bible says that we should be the head and not the tail. We shall be above and not beneath, we shall be the first and not the last, and there is something wrong. You must enter the war room and lift petitions, lamentations, and supplications unto God and take the matter to the court of heaven, and make your case by giving strong arguments on why you have to pass that exam. I am talking about bringing your destiny before the Almighty God in the court of heaven. Deuteronomy 28:13 says, "And the LORD will make you the head and not the tail; you shall be above only, and not be beneath, if you heed the commandments of the LORD your God, which I command you today, and are careful to observe them."

Bring your marriage, family, children, career, ministry, health, and finances to the court of heaven, and state your case and make strong arguments on why you must prevail. The Bible says that the scepter of the wicked shall not rest on the land of the righteous.

When you look at your life and when you look at your family and everything that is around you, it seems that the scepter of the wicked is upon you. In other words, it is an abominable and a detestable thing for the scepter of the wicked to rest on the land of the righteous because that will cause the righteous to sin against God. Psalm 125:3 says, "For the scepter of wickedness shall not rest on the land allotted to the righteous, Lest the righteous reach out their hands to iniquity."

There are satanic entities that are contesting against the council of God in our lives, cities, and nations. That is why as believers we must always be vigilant and watchful to be able to discern the strategic plans of the enemy. We must enter the war room and take our case to the court of heaven to prevail over the satanic kingdom. You must examine yourself (physically and spiritually) often to ensure that you are living a life that is in alignment with the scriptures. Remember God will not bless you if you are not living a life according to his principles. Beloved, remember to pray without ceasing and seek the kingdom of God above all else and live righteously, and you will prevail in the war room thou sayeth the Lord. Amen!

Chapter 8

Prevailing Faith

Often we convince ourselves that we will exercise faith only when necessary to deal with certain situations that occur in our lives. For example, if a loved one becomes terminally ill or a friend was involved in a vehicular accident, we begin to pray and ask God for divine intervention. Beloved, there is no such thing as we will have faith when the time comes, future tense, or we had faith, past tense. The Bible made us understand that faith is always in the present tense or in the now. So if we are going to receive our breakthrough, restoration, and manifestation, it must happen by possessing the *now faith* which is present continuous. If we want testimonies of God's grace and power, it can happen if we have the now faith or prevailing faith. Our prevailing faith is what connects us to our testimonies, breakthroughs, healings, and miracles, not our tears (sorrow). In the absence of faith, our tears are a waste of time. We must weep and cry on the platform of faith for God to respond. There are many of us who are crying over the things that we have lost, the things that the enemy has stolen from us, but tears don't move God if it doesn't come from a place of faith. Hebrew 11:1 states, "Now faith is the substance of things hoped for, the evidence of things not seen."

Prevailing faith means that something must happen on our behalf because miracles are as natural to God as eating is natural to human beings. If we possess prevailing faith, it should not be a surprise when our miracles and breakthroughs occur because it is the Almighty God Jehovah in whom we put our faith, hope, trust, and confidence. Prevailing faith will not disappoint us; prevailing faith will stop the shame and reproach. Prevailing faith will negate the spirit of poverty and lack over our lives. Prevailing faith will make a jobless man have a job. Prevailing faith will make a barren woman fruitful. Prevailing faith is not empty or a psychological state of mind. It is a substance. Faith is tangible. You can take it. If faith is a substance, it means that faith is practicable. The Bible said, "Show me your faith by your works." It means that we don't imagine faith;

we execute faith. It is an action word. James 2:18 says, "But someone will say, 'You have faith, and I have works.' Show me your faith without your works, and I will show you my faith by my works."

What is prevailing faith? It is the uncompromising faith of men that provokes the supernatural intervention of God in the affairs of men, not the tears, complaints, or excuses. Prevailing faith speaks from your innermost being (heart, soul). Everybody is saying different things than what you believe, but you are determined not to adhere to what the present circumstances and situations appear to be; you are only moved by your faith. Prevailing faith connects you to heaven, to your miracles, to your destiny, to your manifestation, to your greatness, to your prophecy, and everything God has planned for you. Prevailing faith cripples the activities of the enemy and paralyzes the doubts that the enemy will attempt to impart upon you. Prevailing faith doesn't get weary, tired, or exhausted. Prevailing faith has no doubts, but it endures. Prevailing faith will give you the tools to recover the things that the enemy has stolen from you. Prevailing faith takes you from the back to the front.

Miracles and breakthroughs are not accidental occurrences; they are the deliberate actions of a man based on his faith that provokes God to move in his favor. There are some of us who have no faith because we are not receiving immediate results. For example, we expect healing and deliverance from that physical infirmity or a new employment opportunity or the restoration of our marriages to occur within a specific time frame, and that timeframe is fast approaching with no immediate results. Then you begin to question God. How can our miracles occur in that narrow time frame? The answer to that question is very simple. If God created the entire universe in six days, he can fix our problem in the twinkle of an eye if we stop doubting and believe that all things are possible through Jesus Christ. Mark 9:23 says, "Jesus said to him, 'If you can believe, all things are possible to him who believes.'"

The Bible said that without faith it is impossible to please God. What triggers or provokes the supernatural to act on our behalf is faith, not complaints. When you have prevailing faith, you don't stop trying until you have overcome the situation. There is no power that can stop you. Faith is not the figment of human imagination or a psychological state of mind. Faith is not the emptiness of thought. Faith is a spiritual entity, force, or power that attracts the attention of the Almighty God. Hebrews11:6

states, "But without faith it is impossible to please Him, for he who comes to God must believe that He is and that He is a rewarder of those who diligently seek Him."

Faith is a living force that draws from a living word (the scriptures) to produce living accounts. In other words, when we have prevailing faith, we have supernatural or a heavenly force. We have the divine intervention that attracts the miracles, our breakthroughs, testimonies, multiplicity, abundance, prosperity, riches, elevation, and promotion. In order for our faith to be prevailing, it must have the living word, solidified by the scriptures. When we are operating on the dimension or platform of prevailing faith, our lives and destinies cannot be stagnant and we cannot be buried. As long as strong faith and prayer are combined, we will be candidates to receive our miracles, breakthroughs, and testimonies. Matthew 21:22 says, "And whatever things you ask in prayer, believing, you will receive."

Jesus said to put your faith and trust in God, not in your own abilities—intelligence, connections, status, credentials, and qualifications, which means that if you place your faith and trust in anything other than God, then your faith is a waste of time. In order for faith to produce desirable results, your faith must be in God because God is the architect of all things (earth, heavens, mankind). In other words, faith and doubt are enemies. Whenever there are doubts, faith dissolves because faith and doubt cannot coexist; they cancel each other out and will not produce any results. Jesus said that if you have faith, you can speak whatever you desire and it will become tangible, visible, physical, and concrete. Faith speaks. You cannot have faith and be silenced. It is imperative that you speak, declare, proclaim, and decree what you desire in order for the manifestation to occur in your timeframe. For example, I am pregnant with twins, I have my own business, or I will own my home. As you speak through the medium of faith, you will see the magnification of what you have spoken. It is called prevailing faith. Mark 11:22–24 says, "So Jesus answered and said to them, 'Have faith in God. For assuredly, I say to you, whoever says to this mountain, "Be removed and be cast into the sea," and does not doubt in his heart, but believes that those things he says will be done, he will have whatever he says. Therefore I say to you, whatever things you ask when you pray, believe that you receive them, and you will have them.'"

A woman who had a flow of blood for twelve years came from behind and touched the hem of Jesus's robe. Jesus said to the woman, "Daughter, your faith has made you well." There were many who were crying for miracles and breakthroughs, but Jesus was not moved by their crying because what moves him is faith. The modern-day church is crying and weeping for miracles, breakthroughs, vindication, and for divine intervention without receiving results because their prayers are void of faith. When you have faith, your destiny, ministry, marriage, career, business, family, and health are well. Where there is faith, you see the move of God and can expect miracles and the supernatural. Mark 5:34 says, "And He said to her, 'Daughter, your faith has made you well. Go in peace, and be healed of your affliction.'"

The blind men were following Jesus and they were tearful, but their weeping did not affect Jesus. Only through faith and belief in Jesus restored their sight. So Jesus was not moved by their loud, incessant crying. He stopped and asked them, "Do you believe?" In other words, do you have faith, do you believe that I am able to heal you? And they responded to him, "Yes, Lord." Then Jesus said, "According to your faith, let it be done as you have desired." Because they believed and had faith in the Lord, their sight was restored. Matthew 9:27–29 states, "When Jesus departed from there, two blind men followed Him, crying out and saying, 'Son of

David, have mercy on us!' And when He had come into the house, the blind men came to Him. And Jesus said to them, 'Do you believe that I am able to do this?' They said to Him, 'Yes, Lord.'

Then He touched their eyes, saying, 'According to your faith let it be to you.'"

Faith comes by hearing the word of God repetitively. You should constantly decree and declare the word of God. A crippled man from Lystra heard Paul speaking. Paul observed him intently and saw that the crippled man had faith to be healed. In other words, Paul did not see his sadness, his sorrow, or the shedding of tears, but he saw his faith. Prevailing faith is what moves God. It makes you irresistible and unstoppable. Your blessing, promotion, pregnancy, should not carry over from year to year. May you be filled with joy and happiness. May you be a part of the people that are laughing, rejoicing, celebrating, jubilating in Jesus's name. Acts 14:8—10 says, "And in Lystra a certain man without strength in his feet was sitting, a cripple from his mother's womb, who had never walked. This man heard Paul speaking. Paul observing him intently and seeing that he had faith to be healed, said with a loud voice, 'stand up straight on your feet!' And he leaped and walked."

Chapter 9

Spiritual War Room

What is a war room? Often people associate a war room with a physical structure such as the Pentagon, a military installation, or a centralized command center. A war room is a secured facility usually higher than the top-secret-security classification level where high-ranking leaders (government, military, federal, or local law enforcement) assemble to develop strategic battle plans and analyze sensitive intelligence data based on foreign, domestic, or global events such as natural disaster or terrorist attack. Within the war room, there are highly sophisticated information systems that provide real-time data regarding the incident such as closed-circuit television, radar, navigations systems, thermal imaging systems, satellite surveillance, and nuclear biological, radiological systems. The war room is a serious place where destinies and lives are decided.

There are two kinds of war rooms, the physical war room and the spiritual war room. The United States government prevails over their enemies in the physical war room, whereas the believers of God (the saints) prevail over their enemies in the spiritual war room. In May 2011, United States President Barack Obama announced that the US military and the CIA operatives located and eliminated the leader of Al Qaeda Osama bin Laden during a raid in Pakistan, where he had taken refuge. As you recall, there were photographs that surfaced globally on social media that depicted President Obama, Vice President Joe Biden, Secretary of State Hillary Clinton, and other military commanders in a room viewing the events on several large video monitors. This specific room is a war room or a situation room explicitly designed for strategic planning and implementation of policies, rules, and regulations. The war room is where destiny is aborted or recovered so there must be clear and concise communications to achieve desirable results; the communication cannot be ambiguous.

It was in the situation room that then president Obama issued the command to eliminate Osama bin Laden from human existence. The commander in chief and his military staff were viewing the events in real-time in the situation room. The Navy Seals entered the compound where bin Laden was hiding; they observed that he was using children and his wives as barriers to shield himself from the attack. The Navy Seal team leader spoke to the commander in chief (President Obama) and asked him for instructions on how to proceed; the commander in chief gave the order to eliminate the target. In other words, when you are given an order from the situation room, you must oblige.

Similarly, a spiritual war room is a place where the saints (believers of Jesus Christ) enter to speak to God. The situation room can be any place where you communicate with God: your church, your vehicle, your office, your home, in your bedroom, or closet. Jesus as your mediator and intercessor will present your prayers to the Almighty who orchestrates divine strategies to fight your battles and defeat your enemies. First Timothy 2:5 says, "For there is one God and one Mediator between God and men, the Man Christ Jesus."

It was in the spiritual war room that the early church received the Holy Spirit. After the resurrection, Jesus said to the disciples, "I am leaving you to join my father in his kingdom, but I will send

the Holy Spirit in my name to comfort, guide, and instruct you."
Jesus told the disciples that they could not receive the Holy Spirit
at their present and physical location. Jesus instructed them to go
to Jerusalem and wait for the Holy Spirit in the spiritual war room
(house, upper room). During Pentecost, the Holy Spirit descended
upon the early church; the disciples and all believers were given
power in the war room. The scriptures say their tongues were like
fire and they were speaking different languages. Acts 2:2–4 states,
"And suddenly there came a sound from heaven, as a rushing
mighty wind, and it filled the whole house where they were sitting.
Then there appeared to them divided tongues, as of fire, and one
sat upon each of them. And they were all filled with the Holy
Spirit and began to speak with other tongues, as the Spirit gave
them utterance."

There are entities that you are fighting that you cannot disarm
by the flesh, you cannot defeat them with your logical abilities,
and you cannot defeat them with your ability to apprehend
and comprehend. You can only defeat them when you enter
the spiritual war room on your knees through prayers. You are
in extreme physical and spiritual pain, you are tired of crying,
walking in shame, and reproach, and you have come to the place

of desperation. You have prayed all kinds of prayers but to no avail, then you must enter the spiritual war room by faith and lift up petitions and supplications to Jehovah to achieve your desired results. Colossians 1:13 states, "He has delivered us from the power of darkness and conveyed us into the kingdom of the Son of His love."

God created the heavens and the earth. God knows the details of your life and all things that the enemy (the kingdom of darkness) is planning against your mission, mandate, and assignment. You must make requests, appeals, lamentations and hold on to the horns of God's holy altar until you recover everything that has eluted your family for years, your generational blessing, your prosperity, your business ventures, ministry, and fruit of the womb. Colossians 1:16 says, "For by Him all things were created that are in heaven and that are on earth, visible and invisible, whether thrones or dominions or principalities or powers. All things were created through Him and for Him."

The spiritual war room is where you are going to have angelic encounters; it is in the war room that you will see the burning bush. It is in the war room where your stained garments are removed, and clean garments are placed upon you. Restoration and deliverance take place in the war room. True worship and humility take place in the war room. I decree and declare that what the enemy has planned and spoken against your relationship, marriage, finances, career, health, ministry, and calling will not prevail in Jesus's name.

Chapter 10

Win Your Battle in the Spiritual War Room by Faith

Great men and women in the Bible have won their battles in the war room. Jesus won the battle to proclaim victory over sin and death in the war room. The apostles interceded and saved Peter's life in the war room. Hannah cried out to God and conceived a male child by the name of Samuel in the war room. Daniel conquered the lions in the war room. Even before he was thrown into the lions' den, he had already prevailed. King Jehoshaphat requested assistance from the Almighty God who gave him the strategic blueprint to defeat the Moabites and their allies all from the war room.

The reason why many believers have lost battles is because they have never entered the spiritual war room. They attempted to solve their issues outside of the war room in the physical realm. We are not fighting against flesh and blood enemies but against spiritual forces of evil that dwell in the heavenly places. Ephesians 6:12 says, "For we do not wrestle against flesh and blood, but against principalities, against powers, against the rulers of the darkness of this age, against spiritual hosts of wickedness in the heavenly places."

Some of you want God and the angels to come down from heaven and drag you into the war room, but they will not force you to enter the war room. You must stop procrastinating and complaining about your conditions, circumstances and enter the war room. It is in the war room that you tell God to let it come to pass that of which he has spoken in your life concerning your destiny, marriage, and family. It is in the war room that you say to God that you are not leaving until he intervenes for divine vindication to change the situation in your favor. It is in the war room that you tell God that you are not leaving until he proves to your enemies that he is alive. It is in the war room that you brag that there is nothing too difficult for your God to do, the God of all impossibilities. All these things happen in the war room, a place of prayers.

Jesus Entered the War Room

Jesus realized the night before his arrest that he must enter the war room. If not, he will not be able to undergo the affliction, pain, suffering, and execution that he was about to endure. So that night he entered the war room, which was in the Garden of Gethsemane at the foot of the Mount of Olives in Jerusalem. Matthews 26:36–38 states, "Then Jesus came with them to a place called Gethsemane, and said to the disciples, 'Sit here while I go and pray over there.' And He took with Him Peter and the two sons of Zebedee, and He began to be sorrowful and deeply distressed. Then He said to them, 'My soul is exceedingly sorrowful, even to death. Stay here and watch with Me.'"

It was in the war room that Jesus began to talk to God and pour out his heart. Jesus kneeled before the Almighty and he said, "Father the mission is heavy. This suffering and affliction that I am about to encounter are too much for me to bear, nevertheless, let thy will be done," so God dispatched an angel to minister, empower and strengthen him for the mission ahead. Luke 22:42–43 says, "Saying, 'Father, if it is Your will, take this cup away from Me; nevertheless, not My will, but Yours, be done.' Then an angel appeared to Him from heaven, strengthening Him."

The Bible made us understand that as Jesus prayed in the Garden of Gethsemane, the war room, the sweat that came from his body was like great drops of blood. In other words, it was in the war room where intense supernatural encounters were occurring which caused Jesus to bleed. Until he shed his blood and died in the war room, he couldn't prevail and accomplish his mandate, mission, and assignment. Jesus won the battle and proclaimed victory over sin and death in the war room. Luke 22:44 says, "And being in agony, He prayed more earnestly. Then His sweat became like great drops of blood falling down to the ground."

Jesus experienced extreme anguish as he prepared to face death. Although he wept to God, asking to be delivered, he was prepared to suffer dishonor and departure from his father. Jesus was ready to perish to fulfill his father's agenda. At times we will undergo trials, not because we want to suffer, but because we want to submit to God's will. Let Jesus's example of compliance withstand and inspire you in times of calamity. You will be able to contend with anything knowing that Jesus Christ is with you. The scriptures say that Jesus will be with us until the end of the age if we obey his commands. Matthew 28:20 says, "I am with you always, even to the end of the age."

The Early Church Interceded for
Apostle Peter in the War Room

The Bible says that Apostle James had been killed by King Herod prematurely, and the people (enemy) were excited and thrilled, so King Herod instructed his soldiers to arrest Apostle Peter to further demonstrate his superiority, power, and authority. King Herod placed Peter in prison and appointed four squads (twelve soldiers) to monitor and guard him to ensure that he does not attempt to flee. King Herod intended to kill Apostle Peter after the festival of unleavened bread (Passover) because according to Jewish customs, you are not supposed to work during the Passover festival.

Now about that time Herod the king stretched out his hand to harass some from the church. Then he killed James the brother of John with the sword. And because he saw that it pleased the Jews, he proceeded further to seize Peter also. Now it was during the Days of Unleavened Bread. So when he had arrested him, he put him in prison, and delivered him to four squads of soldiers to keep him, intending to bring him before the people after Passover. Peter was therefore kept in prison, but constant prayer was offered to God for him by the church. And when Herod was about to bring him out, that night Peter was sleeping, bound with two chains between two soldiers; and the guards before the door were keeping the prison. (Acts 12:1–6)

When the apostle James was killed, the early church did not enter the war room because they were taken by surprise that is why the apostle James lost his life prematurely; however, when King Herod had Peter arrested, the early church was alert, prepared, and determined to intercede for the apostle Peter. They passionately refused to allow the apostle Peter to suffer the same fate as Apostle James. They entered the war room in the presence of God and prayed without ceasing for him. They directly addressed the spirit of Herod by saying, "You are a murdering spirit, a spirit of assassination, a spirit that aborts destines impulsively and what you have planned for Apostle Peter will not stand." They declared and spoke counter declarations to the kingdom of darkness and they refused to allow the apostle Peter to suffer the same fate as Apostle James.

The church negotiated and bargained with God, and victory was achieved in the war room. God said, "Because you have come into the war room, that which you have requested and petitioned has been granted." Immediately, an angel was dispatched into the prison. The angel walked into the prison not in the realm of the flesh but in the realm of the spirit. If you are going to win the battle of life, you must win it in the realm of the spirit. Until you overcome in the realm of the spirit, you will not succeed in the realm of the flesh. The angel could have been dispatched into the prison in the realm of the flesh, but the angel came through the realm of the spirit. That was why the twelve soldiers couldn't see or locate him. They never realized that somebody has entered the prison and removed the shackles and chains from Peter. Peter walked out of the prison alive and well; what King Herod planned against Peter did not prevail.

The Bible said that King Herod sat on his throne and wore his royal apparel (regalia, ceremonial garment) and began giving his speech. During his speech, the people were shouting, hailing, and screaming, saying, "This is not the voice of a man. This is the voice of God," referring to King Herod. And God said, "I will let you and the people know that I have just rendered a verdict in the war room after hearing the cry of my children. I have just granted their request and so I am going to let you and the people know that you are a man of flesh and what you intended to do against Apostle Peter has been reversed." Suddenly, King Herod was immediately struck and died, and worms devoured his body. This has never happened before in the presence of the multitude. Acts 12:21–23 states, "So on a set day Herod, arrayed in royal apparel, sat on his throne, and gave an oration to them. And the people kept shouting, 'The voice of a god and not of a man!' Then immediately an angel of the Lord struck him, because he did not give glory to God. And he was eaten by worms and died."

Satan attacks you because you never go into the war room. It is about time that you enter the war room and take an offensive approach against the kingdom of darkness, to decree and declare God's purpose for your life, marriage, career, and destiny. You must enter the war room with purpose and determination by holding on to the horns of the altar and crying out to the Almighty God. You don't leave until you receive a solution, remedy, divine intervention and the situation has been turned around in your favor. Jeremiah 29:11–12 says, "For I know the thoughts that I think toward you, says the LORD, thoughts of peace and not of evil, to give you a future and a hope. Then you will call upon Me and go and pray to Me, and I will listen to you."

There are so many of us who are dealing with difficult and challenging situations outside of the war room in the physical realm and that is why we are not receiving solutions to our problems. We must enter the war room to contend with the forces of darkness that are fighting against our destinies and prophecies. In the war room, the Holy Spirit provides you with the tools, weapons, and techniques to destroy and disarm your enemies. Luke 12:12 says, "For the Holy Spirit will teach you in that very hour what you ought to say."

Hannah Entered Shiloh for a Child in the War Room

And whenever the time came for Elkanah to make an offering, he would give portions to Peninnah his wife and to all her sons and daughters. But to Hannah he would give a double portion, for he loved Hannah, although the LORD had closed her womb. And her rival also provoked her severely, to make her miserable, because the LORD had closed her womb. So it was, year by year, when she went up to the house of the LORD, that she provoked her; therefore, she wept and did not eat. Then Elkanah her husband said to her, "Hannah, why do you weep? Why do you not eat? And why is your heart grieved? Am I not better to you than ten sons?" Once after a sacrificial meal at Shiloh, Hannah got up and went to pray. Eli the priest was sitting at his customary place beside the entrance of the Tabernacle. Hannah was in deep anguish, crying bitterly as she prayed to the LORD. And she made this vow: "O LORD of Heaven's Armies, if you will look upon my sorrow and answer my prayer and give me a son, then I will give him back to you. He will be yours for his entire lifetime, and as a sign that he has been dedicated to the LORD, his hair will never be cut." As she was praying to the LORD, Eli watched her. Seeing her lips moving but hearing no sound, he thought she had been drinking. (1 Sam. 1:4–13)

The Bible says that Hannah had a rival by the name of Peninnah. Peninnah was evil. She constantly spoke curse words against her. Peninnah was fierce and relentless in her attack on Hannah; she also called her barren because she was not able to conceive a child. In those days if a woman could not bear children, she was considered worthless or a nonentity. Hannah couldn't take it any longer; she was sick and tired of being humiliated and barren, so she decided to enter the war room at Shiloh, the temple of God. When she entered the war room, she lifted a lamination to Jehovah (God). She began to agonize and travail in prayer.

There are various dimensions of prayer; however, there is a specific level that you rise to that no one can articulate with words, only the Lord can discern. You begin to groan in the spirit; groaning in the spirit means that you are on a higher level of prayer where words are not sufficient. No man understands the sounds but Jehovah, our Almighty God. That is why sometimes, people shout, "Hey, hey." Nobody understands when you say, "Hey, hey," but Jehovah who created sounds understands what you are saying.

Hannah went to the war room and began negotiating with Jehovah. She said, "God, you need a prophet because there is no prophet in Israel. I need a son, give me a son and I will dedicate him to you as your prophet, and he will serve you for his entire life." In other words, the war room is where negotiation occurs. God heard what Hannah said in the war room, and God accepted the proposition, "I will give you a son and you will give me a prophet." And the Bible said that Hannah walked out of Shiloh, and one year later she conceived a male child. She named him Samuel. She brought him to the same war room where the commander in chief (God) accepted the terms of the contract and she said, "Jehovah, you have fulfilled your part of the contract, and now I have come to fulfill my part. This is your prophet. He will live in the war room for the rest of his life." Contracts are won in the war room. Destines are turned around in the war room. Healing takes place in the war room; barrenness is eradicated in the war room. Shame is turned upside down for glory in the war room. Heavy grief and hopelessness are taken away, and a new garment of praise is placed upon you in the war room.

Daniel Prevailed over the Lion in the War Room

Now when Daniel knew that the writing was signed, he went home. And in his upper room, with his windows open toward Jerusalem, he knelt down on his knees three times that day, and prayed and gave thanks before his God, as was his custom since early days. Then these men assembled and found Daniel praying and making supplication before his God. And they went before the king, and spoke concerning the king's decree: "Have you not signed a decree that every man who petitions any god or man within thirty days, except you, O king, shall be cast into the den of lions?" (Dan. 6:10–12)

Daniel went on his knees three times a day and prayed and gave thanks before his God; this was his custom since the early days. Daniel had favor with King Darius, so he appointed him to a high position over all the other governors in the province. The other governors became envious and very angry, so they conspired against Daniel. Daniel was trustworthy and he handled all government affairs that were entrusted to him with honesty and integrity. His conspirators could not find any fault in him. So they petitioned the king to sign an order that stated if anyone prays to any other god, divine or human, except King Darius in the next thirty days will be thrown into the lion's den. The conspirators manipulated King Darius to apply his signature to the decree to entrap Daniel.

When Daniel discovered that the King signed the decree, he entered the war room. Daniel opened his windows in the direction of Jerusalem; he knelt on his knees in the upper room because the commander in chief (God) was always there to answers prayers. The governors responded to Daniel's location and discovered that he was praying, which violated the king's order. The governors informed King Darius that Daniel disobeyed his orders. King Darius gave the order to arrest Daniel and threw him into the lion's den.

The next morning King Darius hurried to the lion's den and called out to Daniel in agony and to his surprise, Daniel was alive and well. Daniel said that the Almighty God sent an angel to close the lions' mouths "for I have been found blameless by his account." Daniel prevailed against his enemies because he prayed in the spirit; he lifted lamentations and supplications before God until he received his breakthrough. He stayed in the war room which was his source of strength and power. Daniel defeated the lions prior to being thrown in the lions' den because he contended with the kingdom of darkness in the war room. Daniel 6:22 says, "My God sent His angel and shut the lions' mouths, so that they have not hurt me, because I was found innocent before Him; and also, O King, I have done no wrong before you."

You cannot go into the war room and not be a carrier of the presence of God. You cannot go into the war room without your spiritual eyes opened to see everything that is occurring in the realms of the spirit around you. Where are the true prayer warriors today that will enter the war room with persistence to receive strategic plans? For example, in that employment interview that you attended, you should already know the outcome because you prevailed in the war room.

King Jehoshaphat Prevailed over the Moabites

It happened after this that the people of Moab with the people of Ammon, and others with them besides the Ammonites, came to battle against Jehoshaphat. Then some came and told Jehoshaphat, saying, "A great multitude is coming against you from beyond the sea, from Syria; and they are in Hazazon Tamar" (which is En Gedi). And Jehoshaphat feared, and set himself to seek the LORD, and proclaimed a fast throughout all Judah. So Judah gathered together to ask help from the LORD; and from all the cities of Judah they came to seek the LORD. Then Jehoshaphat stood in the assembly of Judah and Jerusalem, in the house of the LORD, before the new court, and said: "O LORD God of our fathers, are You not God in heaven, and do You not rule over all the kingdoms of the nations, and in Your hand is there not power and might, so that no one is able to withstand You? Are You not our God, who drove out the inhabitants of this land before Your people Israel, and gave it to the descendants of Abraham Your friend forever?" (2 Chron. 20:1–7)

The Moabites, their allies, and multiple nations were planning to attack the kingdom of Israel. Jehoshaphat the king of Israel was petrified because they were severely outnumbered. So King Jehoshaphat entered the war room and asked God for divine intervention. "Are you not sovereign? Are you not the ancient of days? Are you not the creator that wasn't created, the Adonai, the El Shaddai? Are you not the God of Abraham, the God of Isaac, and the God of Jacob? Are you not the God that rules in the affairs of men and over all kingdoms and nations of the earth? Will you watch these uncircumcised nations obliterate your people? Will you watch for the enemy of your son to rejoice? Let not their predictions and their projections against your son and your church manifest."

King Jehoshaphat stayed in the war room and made petitions unto the Lord until he received his strategic battle plans. God spoke to him in the war room and said, "Don't let the military march forward in attack formation." The Lord instructed King Jehoshaphat to assemble the choir from the temple with their trumpets, drums, and cymbals. Let them go ahead of the armies that have swords, armor, and chariots. The choir played music and sang songs of praises while marching into the camp of the enemies. And before they arrived, God and his angels orchestrated an ambush against all their enemies. In logical human thinking, this does not make sense, and we will surely perish based on this plan, but this type of strategy and technique to defeat the enemy only comes from the spiritual war room. Second Chronicles 20:21–22 states, "And when he had consulted with the people, he appointed those who should sing to the Lord, and who should praise the beauty of holiness, as they went out before the army and were saying: 'Praise the Lord, For His mercy endures forever.' Now when they began to sing and to praise, the Lord set ambushes against the people of Ammon, Moab and Mount Seir, who had come against Judah; and they were defeated."

When Jehoshaphat and his people entered the city, they found all their enemies dead; the Lord fought their battle and gave them a triumphant victory. There is nowhere in scriptures that states the army or the choir fought against the enemy. For three days King Jehoshaphat and his army collected and plundered all the resources of the enemy which included gold and silver; there was so much that they could not carry it all. They took as much as they desired, and no one opposed or resisted them. Second Chronicles 20:25 says, "When Jehoshaphat and his people came to take away their spoil, they found among them an abundance of valuables on the dead bodies, and precious jewelry, which they stripped off for themselves, more than they could carry away; and they were three days gathering the spoil because there was so much."

Any enemy that is holding onto your valuables, they will die holding on to it. And you will stand by their dead bodies and take your valuables from them. Only the people that have entered the war room and stayed in the war room will understand the language of the spirit. You must enter the war room by faith to receive your strategic plan from God to gain victory. In Jesus's mighty name, we pray. Amen!

Lightning Source UK Ltd.
Milton Keynes UK
UKHW010737110621
385337UK00001B/87